Published in 2020

All pages and text in this book

belong to

Christopher Merton.

This book belongs to:

For Joe

Deep,

Deep,

Deep,

into the forest

Sits a very big rock.

Much

deeper

into

the forest

You'll find the sloooooowest animal in the whole forest. Mr. Sloth.

"My Birthday is on Friday.
I am very excited to Invite
all of my friends
over for a party."

"Hello Mr. Fox, would you like to come to my party on Friday?"

"Yes I would love to come."

"Oh, hi Rock. looks like it is going take
A very long time climb over you."

"Yes I would love to come,
I will make a banner."

"Hello Mrs. Llama, would you like to
Come to my party on Friday?"

"Yes, that sounds fun. I will bring
Some party hats."

"Good evening Mr. Anteater. Would you like to come to my party on Friday"

"Oh yes. I do love to dance.
I will bring some music"

"Hello Mr. Toucan, Would you like to Come to my party on Friday?"

"Mr. Sloth, today is Friday!"

"OH no,
I won't make
It back in
Time for my
party.
I am too
Sloooow!

"Do not
Worry,
I have some

balloons

and a

great
Idea."

Mr. Toucan flies Mr. Sloth back to his party.

Mr. Sloth makes it back just in Time to celebrate.

Mr. Sloth was so happy that he got to 'hang out' with all his friends on his birthday.

Christopher Merton
is an Irish based
Illustrator, writer
and designer.

cmerton_design

Printed in Poland
by Amazon Fulfillment
Poland Sp. z o.o., Wrocław